carta's

CONCISE

BIBLE
ATLAS

carta's

CONCISE
BIBLE
ATLAS

carta

THE ISRAEL MAP AND PUBLISHING COMPANY LTD

ISBN 965-220-001-8

Printed in Israel

CONTENTS

CHRONOLOGICAL TABLE

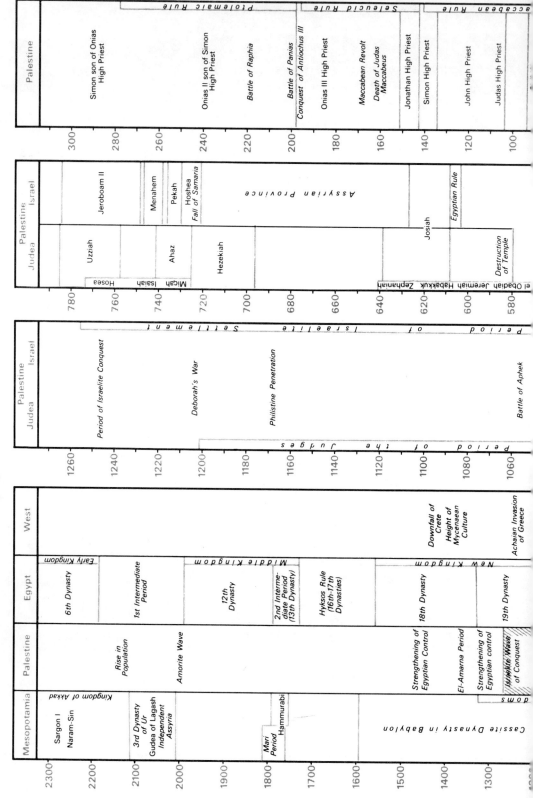

Panel (1100 B.C. – 100 A.D.)

Dates: 1100, 1000, 900, 800, 700, 600, 500, 400, 300, 200, 100, B.C., A.D., 100

Left column events:
- 20th Dynasty
- Dorian Invasion of Greece
- 21st Dynasty
- 22nd Dynasty
- Etruscan Invasion of Italy
- Homer
- First Olympic Games
- 23rd-25th Dynasties
- Assyrian Conquest
- Height of Etruscan Culture
- 26th Dynasty
- Roman Republic Established
- Persian Wars
- Herodotus
- Decline of Athens
- Persian Conquest
- 28th-30th Dynasties
- Persian Rule
- Punic Wars
- Hannibal
- Roman Rule in Greece
- Caesar
- Roman Empire
- Ptolemaic Rule
- Seleucid Rule
- Roman Rule

Middle band events:
- Institution of Kingship in Israel
- Divided Monarchy
- Destruction of Samaria and Exile of Israel
- Destruction of Jerusalem and Exile of Judah
- Restoration of Zion
- Conquests of Alexander the Great
- Ptolemaic Rule
- Seleucid Rule
- Maccabeans
- King Herod
- Birth of Jesus
- Destruction of Second Temple

Lower band empires:
- Minor
- Assyrian Empire
- Babylonian Empire
- Persian Empire
- Conquests of Alexander the Great
- Seleucid Rule
- Parthian Empire
- Parthian Wars

Panel (1020 – 800 B.C.)

Dates: 1020, 1000, 980, 960, 940, 920, 900, 880, 860, 840, 820, 800

- Saul
- David
- Solomon
- Rehoboam
- Jeroboam son of Nebat
- Baasha
- Asa
- Ahab
- Jehoshaphat
- Jehu
- Jehoash
- Amaziah

Prophets: Elijah, Elisha, Jonah, Amos

Panel (540 – 320 B.C.)

Dates: 540, 520, 500, 480, 460, 440, 420, 400, 380, 360, 340, 320

Header (rotated): Satrapies of the Persians — Wars of Diodachi

- Isaiah 40
- Zechariah Haggai
- Malachi
- Ezra
- Nehemiah
- Conquered by Alexander
- Overrun by Antigonus
- Overrun by Ptolemy I

Panel (60 B.C. – 160 A.D.)

Dates: 60, 40, 20, B.C., A.D., 20, 40, 60, 80, 100, 120, 140, 160

Header (rotated): Roman Rule

- Hyrcanus II High Priest
- Siege of Pompey
- Parthian Invasion
- Reign of Herod
- Birth of Jesus
- Archelaus
- Philip Antipas
- Jesus' Ministry
- Agrippa I King of Judea
- Ministry of Apostles
- First Jewish Revolt
- Destruction of Jerusalem
- Fall of Masada
- Jewish Centre at Jannia
- Bar Kokhba Revolt
- Fall of Bethther
- Spread of Christianity
- First Procurators
- Later Procurators
- Agrippa II

TO THE READER

This Atlas has been specially designed to help you understand and enjoy the Bible. Although it is concise and easy to follow you will discover that it is packed with information. An index with almost 900 entries makes all this material instantly available.

The maps and city plans tell you about places and frontiers and distances at every period of Bible history. The illustrations provide fascinating archaeological and cultural data. A time chart relates the different strands of Bible history to what was going on elsewhere in the ancient world.

From the Atlas you can learn about the commerce of the ancient Near East, the wanderings of ancient peoples, the major travel routes and the rise of Christianity. It has been researched and produced by specialists to bring a new dimension to your study of the Bible

The Publishers

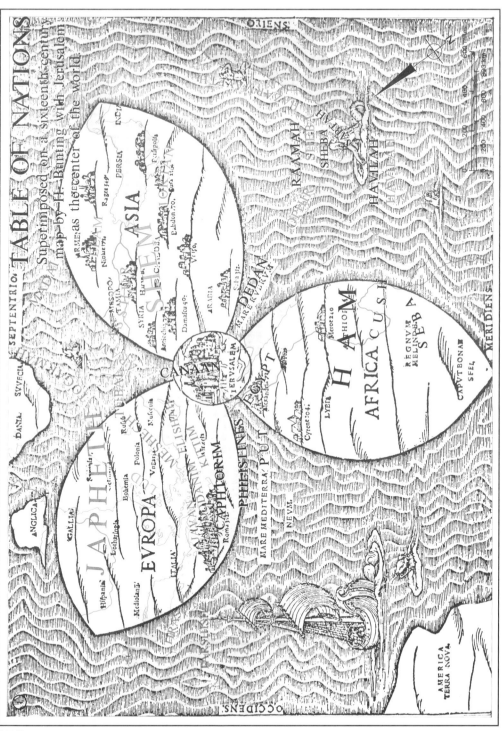

TABLE OF NATIONS

Superimposed on a sixteenth-century
map by H. Bunting with Jerusalem
as the center of the world.

© carta

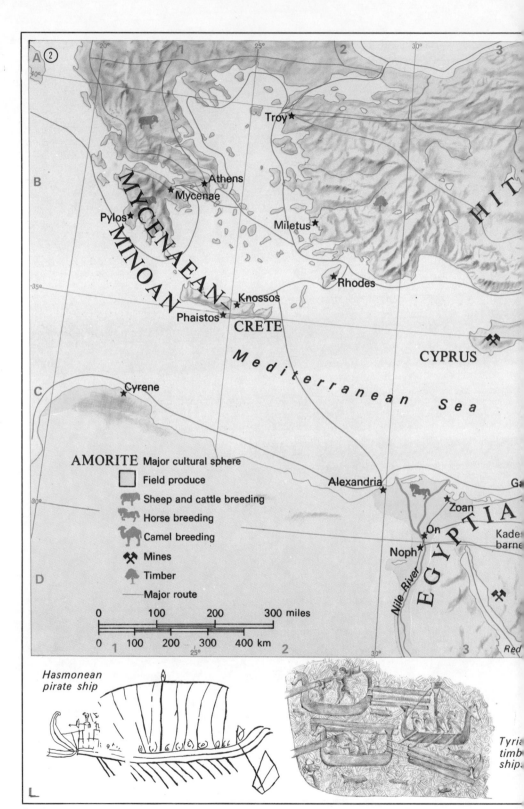

A ②

Troy★

MYCENAEAN-

Athens★
Mycenae★

Pylos★

MINOAN

Miletus★

Rhodes★

Knossos★
Phaistos★

CRETE

Mediterranean Sea

HIT...

CYPRUS

Cyrene★

AMORITE Major cultural sphere
☐ Field produce
🐃 Sheep and cattle breeding
🐎 Horse breeding
🐪 Camel breeding
⚒ Mines
🌳 Timber
— Major route

Alexandria★

Zoan★
On★

Ga...

Kade...
barne...

Noph★

EGYPT...

Nile River

0   100   200   300 miles
0 100 200 300 400 km

Hasmonean
pirate ship

Tyria...
timb...
ship...

© carta

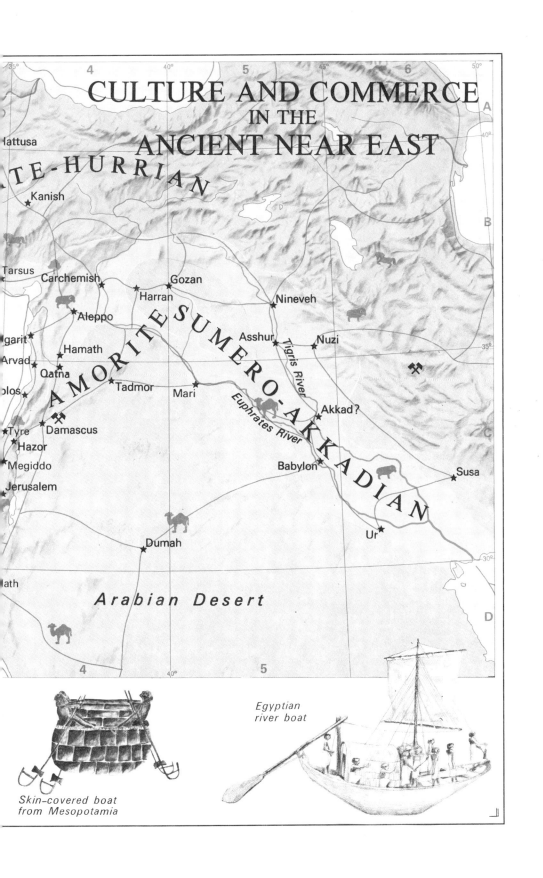

CULTURE AND COMMERCE
IN THE
ANCIENT NEAR EAST

Hattusa

TE-HURRIAN

Kanish

Tarsus

Carchemish Gozan

Harran

Aleppo

Nineveh

garit

Hamath Asshur Nuzi

Arvad

Qatna

olos

Tadmor Mari Akkad?

Tyre Damascus

Hazor

Megiddo Babylon Susa

Jerusalem

Ur

Dumah

ath

Arabian Desert

Tigris River

Euphrates River

AMORITE

SUMERO-AKKADIAN

*Egyptian
river boat*

*Skin-covered boat
from Mesopotamia*

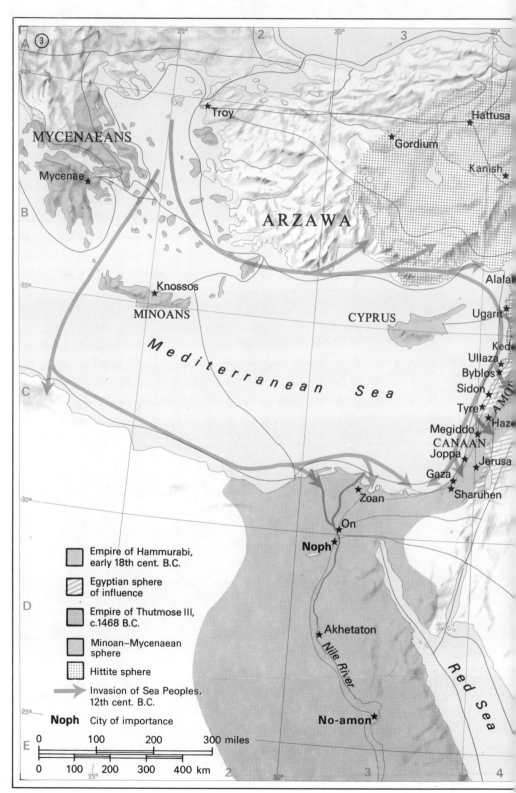

A
③
25°   2   30°   3   35°

Troy★

Hattusa★

MYCENAEANS
                                        ★Gordium
Mycenae★
                                                      Kanish★

B   ARZAWA

40°
35°

Alala

★Knossos   Ugarit★

MINOANS   CYPRUS   Ked•
                                                     Ullaza★
                                            M e d i t e r r a n e a n   S e a
                                                     Byblos★
                                                     Sidon•
C   Tyre★   AMOR
                                                             ★Haz•
                                            Megiddo★
                                            CANAAN
                                            Joppa★   Jerusa
                                                 Gaza★
30°   Zoan★   ★Sharuhen

On★

Noph★

D
☐ Empire of Hammurabi,
  early 18th cent. B.C.

▨ Egyptian sphere
  of influence

☐ Empire of Thutmose III,
  c.1468 B.C.   ★Akhetaton

☐ Minoan–Mycenaean
  sphere

▦ Hittite sphere

➜ Invasion of Sea Peoples,
  12th cent. B.C.

25°
Noph City of importance   **No-amon**★

E 0   100   200   300 miles
   ┣━━━━┿━━━━┿━━━━┿━━━━┫
   0   100 200 300 400 km
       25°   2   30°   3   4

© carta

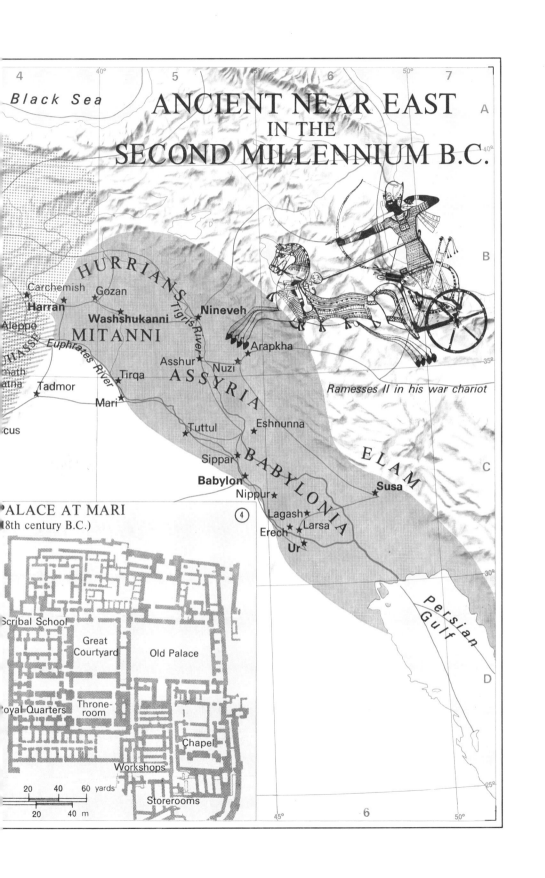

4   40°   5   6   50°   7

Black Sea

A

ANCIENT NEAR EAST
IN THE
SECOND MILLENNIUM B.C.

40°

B

HURRIANS

Carchemish ★ Gozan ★

Harran ★ **Washshukanni** ★ **Nineveh** ★

Aleppo ★ MITANNI *Tigris River*

★IASSE *Euphrates River* Asshur ★ Arapkha ★

nath Tirqa ★ A S S Y R I A Nuzi ★

atna Tadmor ★ Mari ★

cus

Ramesses II in his war chariot

35°

Tuttul ★ Eshnunna ★

E L A M

C

Sippar ★ B A B Y L O N I A

Babylon ★ **Susa** ★

Nippur ★

PALACE AT MARI
(8th century B.C.)

④

Lagash ★ Larsa ★

Erech ★

Ur ★

30°

Persian Gulf

```
Scribal School

Great
Courtyard        Old Palace

Royal Quarters   Throne-
                 room

                 Chapel

Workshops

20    40    60 yards

20      40 m        Storerooms
```

D

25°

45°   6   50°

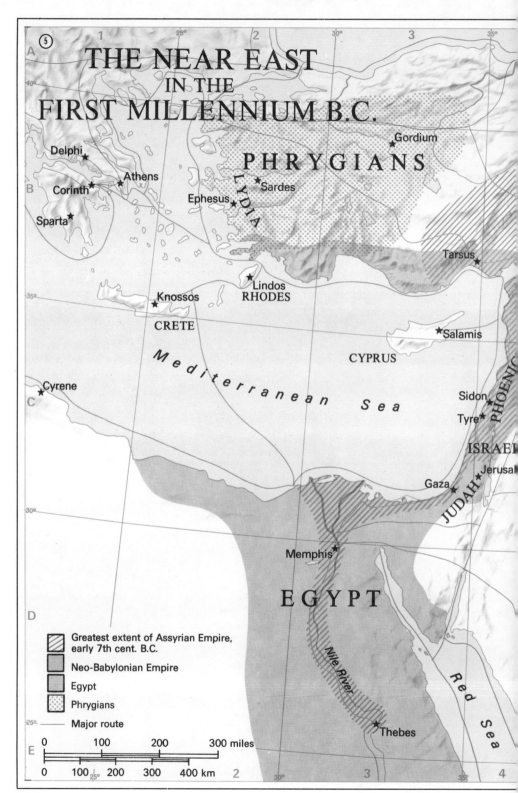

THE NEAR EAST
IN THE
FIRST MILLENNIUM B.C.

PHRYGIANS

Gordium

Delphi

Athens
Corinth
Sparta

LYDIA
Sardes
Ephesus

Tarsus

Lindos
RHODES

Knossos

CRETE

Salamis

CYPRUS

Mediterranean Sea

Cyrene

Sidon
Tyre
PHOENIC

ISRAEL
Jerusa

Gaza
JUDAH

Memphis

EGYPT

Nile River

Red Sea

Greatest extent of Assyrian Empire,
early 7th cent. B.C.

Neo-Babylonian Empire

Egypt

Phrygians

Major route

| 0 | 100 | 200 | 300 miles |

| 0 | 100 | 200 | 300 | 400 km |

Thebes

© carta

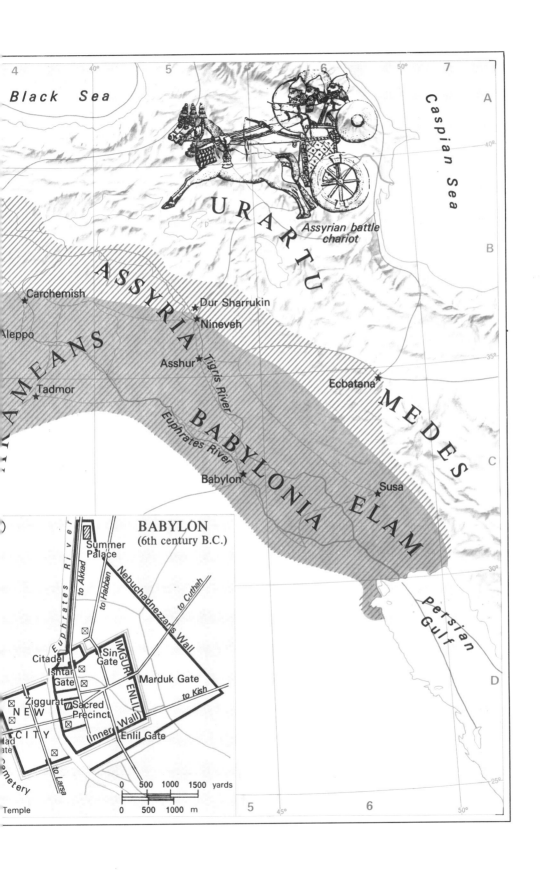

Black Sea

Caspian Sea

URARTU

Assyrian battle
chariot

ASSYRIA

Carchemish

Dur Sharrukin

Nineveh

Aleppo

ARAMEANS

Asshur

Tigris River

Tadmor

Ecbatana

MEDES

BABYLONIA

Euphrates River

Babylon

ELAM

Susa

Persian Gulf

BABYLON
(6th century B.C.)

Euphrates River

Summer
Palace

to Akkad

to Habban

Nebuchadnezzar's Wall

to Cuthah

Citadel

Sin
Gate

IMGUR ENLIL

Ishtar
Gate

Marduk Gate

to Kish

Ziggurat

NEW

Sacred
Precinct

(Inner Wall)

Enlil Gate

CITY

to Larsa

Temple

Cemetery

| 0 | 500 | 1000 | 1500 | yards |

| 0 | 500 | 1000 | m |

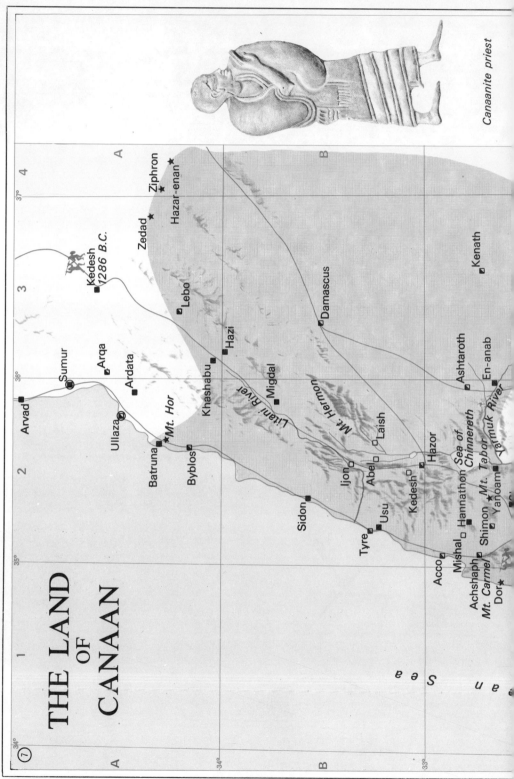

THE LAND
OF
CANAAN

Canaanite priest

Arvad

Sumur
Arqa
Ardata
Ullaza
Batruna
★ Mt. Hor
Byblos
Khashabu
Hazi
Sidon
Litani River
Migdal
Mt. Hermon
Laish
Hazor
Ijon
Abel
Kedesh
Usu
Tyre
Acco
Mishal
Hannathon
Achshaph
Mt. Carmel
Shimon
Dor ★
Yanoam
Sea of
Chinnereth
Mt. Tabor
Yarmuk River
Ashtaroth
En-anab
Kenath
Damascus
Lebo
Kedesh
1286 B.C.
Zedad ★
Ziphron ★
Hazar-enan ★

Sea

© carta

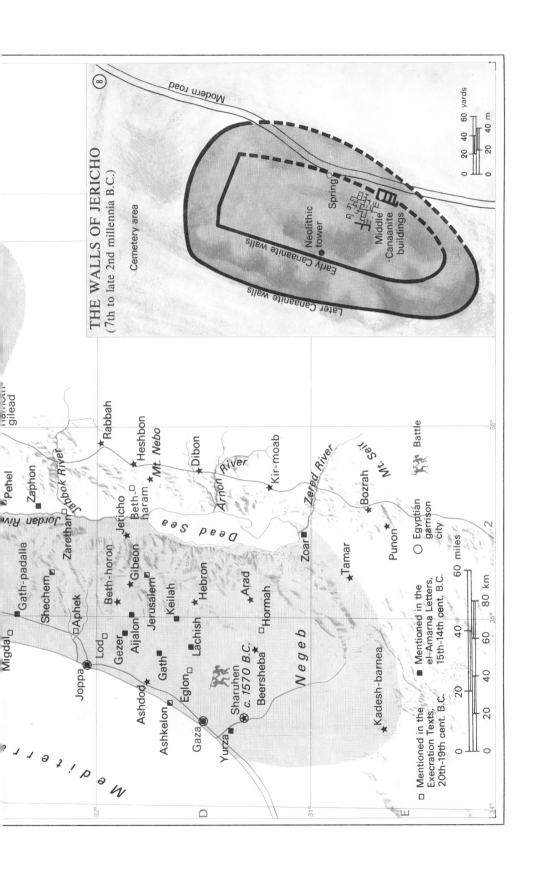

THE WALLS OF JERICHO
(7th to late 2nd millennia B.C.)

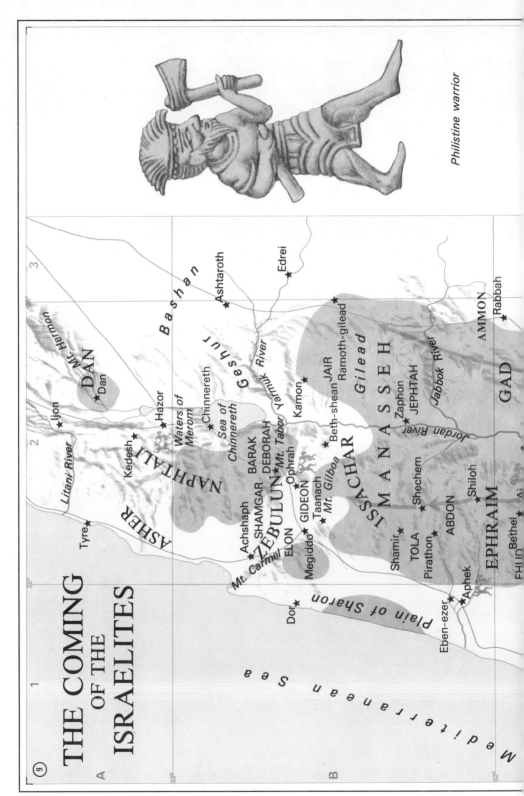

THE COMING
OF THE
ISRAELITES

Philistine warrior

Mediterranean Sea

Plain of Sharon

Mt. Carmel

Dor

Megiddo

ASHER

Tyre

Litani River

Ijon

Kedesh

Achshaph

SHAMGAR

ZEBULUN

ELON

GIDEON

NAPHTALI

DAN

Dan

Mt. Hermon

Hazor

Waters of
Merom

Chinnereth

Sea of
Chinnereth

BARAK

DEBORAH

Mt. Tabor

Ophrah

Taanach

Mt. Gilboa

ISSACHAR

Shamir,

TOLA

Pirathon

Aphek

Eben-ezer

EPHRAIM

Bethel

Shiloh

ABDON

Shechem

MANASSEH

Zaphon

JEPHTAH

Beth-shean

Kamon

Yarmuk River

Gilead

JAIR

Ramoth-gilead

Bashan

Geshur

Ashtaroth

Edrei

Jabbok River

Jordan River

GAD

AMMON

Rabbah

© carta

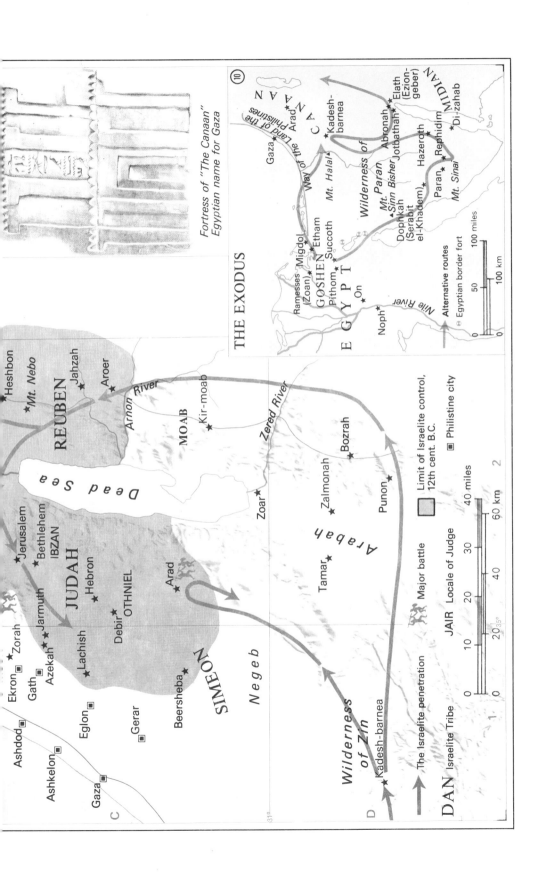

Fortress of "The Canaan"
Egyptian name for Gaza

THE EXODUS ⑩

CANAAN

Gaza
Way of the Land of the Philistines
Arad
Kadesh-barnea
Mt. Halal
Abronah
Elath (Ezion-geber)
MIDIAN
Di-zahab
Wilderness of Paran
Jotbathah
Hazeroth
Mt. Sinn Bisher
Rephidim
Paran
Mt. Sinai
Dophkah (Serabit el-Khadem)

Migdol
Ramesses (Zoan)
Etham
Succoth
GOSHEN
Pithom
On
E G Y P T
Noph

Nile River

⊕ Egyptian border fort
→ Alternative routes

0   50   100 miles
0   100 km

Heshbon
Mt. Nebo
Jahzah
Aroer
REUBEN

Arnon River

Dead Sea

MOAB
Kir-moab

Zered River

Zoar
Bozrah

Tamar
Zalmonah
Araba
Punon

Ekron
Zorah
Gath
Azekah
Jarmuth
Jerusalem
Bethlehem
IBZAN
JUDAH
Hebron
Debir
OTHNIEL
Lachish
Arad
Ashdod
Eglon
Gerar
Beersheba
SIMEON
Negeb
Ashkelon
Gaza

Wilderness of Zin
Kadesh-barnea

Limit of Israelite control, 12th cent. B.C.
■ Philistine city
🏃 Major battle
→ The Israelite penetration
DAN Israelite Tribe   JAIR Locale of Judge

0   10   20   30   40 miles
0   20   40   60 km
35°

C

D

1   2

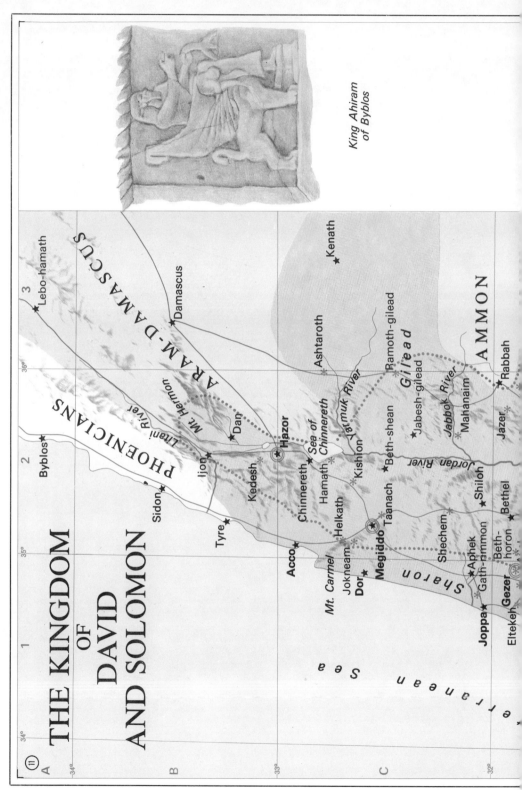

THE KINGDOM
OF
DAVID
AND SOLOMON

King Ahiram
of Byblos

PHOENICIANS

ARAM-DAMASCUS

AMMON

Gilead

Sharon

Mediterranean Sea

Byblos

Lebo-hamath

Damascus

Sidon

Ijon

Dan

Kenath

Tyre

Kedesh

Hazor

Ashtaroth

Chinnereth

Sea of
Chinnereth

Ramoth-gilead

Acco

Helkath

Hamath

Kishon

Beth-shean

Jabesh-gilead

Mahanaim

Jazer

Rabbah

Mt. Carmel

Jokneam

Taanach

Jordan River

Dor

Megiddo

Shechem

Shiloh

Aphek

Bethel

Gath-rimmon

Beth-
horon

Joppa

Gezer

Eltekeh

Mt. Hermon

Litani River

Yarmuk River

Jabbok River

① 11

A

B

C

34°

35°

36°

34°

33°

32°

1

2

3

© carta

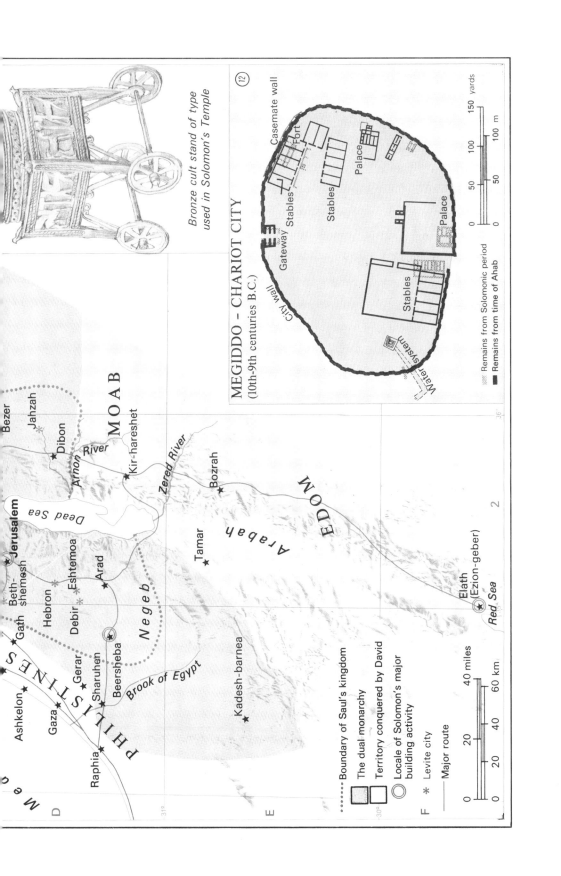

Bronze cult stand of type
used in Solomon's Temple

⑫

MEGIDDO – CHARIOT CITY
(10th–9th centuries B.C.)

Casemate wall

Fort

Gateway

Stables

Stables

Palace

Palace

City wall

Stables

Water
system

▨ Remains from Solomonic period

▬ Remains from time of Ahab

0   50   100   150   yards

0   50   100   m

MOAB

Bezer

Jahzah ✶

Dibon ★

Arnon River

Kir-haresheth ★

Zered River

Bozrah ★

EDOM

Dead Sea

Tamar ★

Arabah

Elath
(Ezion-geber) ⊚
Red Sea

Jerusalem

Beth-
shemesh ✶
Gath ★

Hebron ★

Debir ✶ Eshtemoa ✶

Arad ★

Negeb

Beersheba ★

Brook of Egypt

Kadesh-barnea ★

Ashkelon ★

Gaza ★

Gerar ★ Sharuhen ★

Raphia ★

PHILISTINES

M e d

·········· Boundary of Saul's kingdom

☐ The dual monarchy

⊚ Territory conquered by David

⊚ Locale of Solomon's major
building activity

✶ Levite city

—— Major route

0   20   40 miles

0   20   40   60 km

D

E

F

2

36°

31°

30°

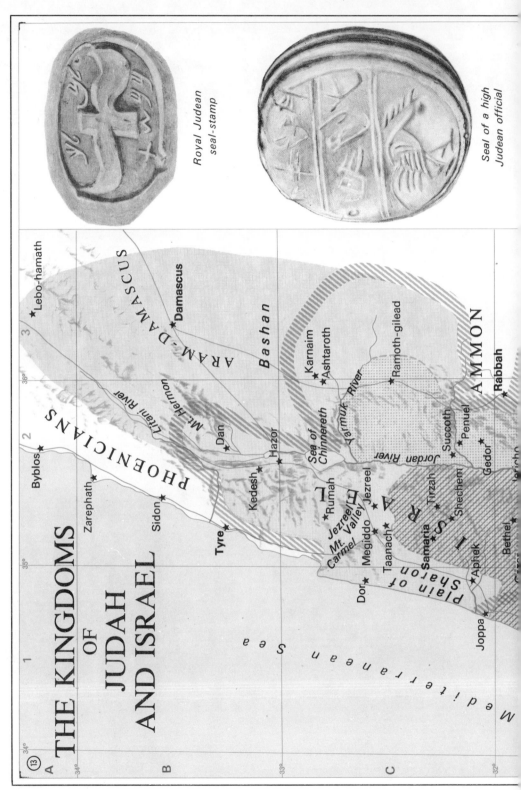

THE KINGDOMS OF JUDAH AND ISRAEL

Royal Judean seal-stamp

Seal of a high Judean official

Lebo-hamath

ARAM-DAMASCUS

Damascus

Bashan

Karnaim
Ashtaroth

Ramoth-gilead

AMMON

Rabbah

PHOENICIANS

Litani River

Mt. Hermon

Dan

Hazor

Sea of Chinnereth

Yarmuk River

Jordan River

Succoth

Penuel

Gedor

Jericho

Byblos

Zarephath

Sidon

Tyre

Kedesh

Rumah

Jezreel

Mt. Carmel
Jezreel Valley

Megiddo
Taanach

Tirzah

Shechem

Samaria

Aphek

ISRAEL

Dor

Plain of Sharon

Joppa

Bethel

Mediterranean Sea

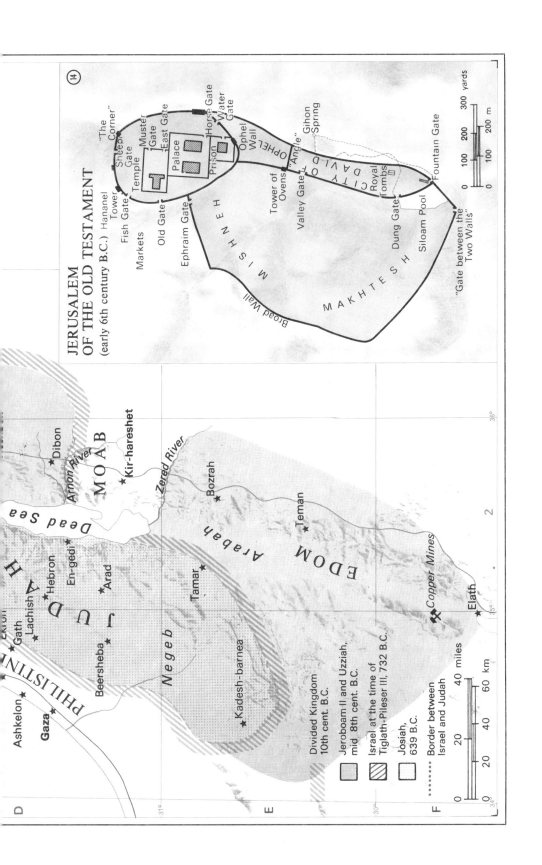

JERUSALEM
OF THE OLD TESTAMENT
(early 6th century B.C.)

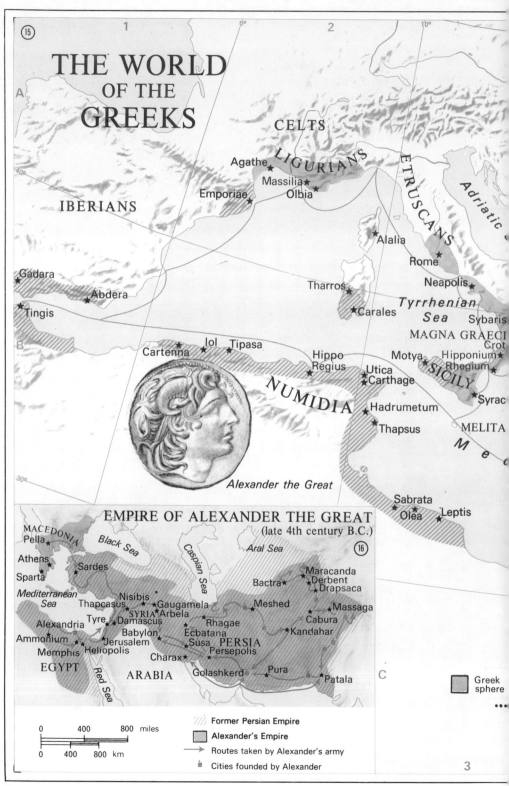

THE WORLD
OF THE
GREEKS

CELTS

LIGURIANS

ETRUSCANS

Adriatic

Agathe

Massilia

Olbia

IBERIANS

Emporiae

Alalia

Rome

Gadara

Tharros

Neapolis

Abdera

Tyrrhenian

Tingis

Carales

Sea

Sybaris

MAGNA GRAECI

Crot

Iol Tipasa

Cartenna

Hippo

Motya Hipponium

Regius

Rhegium

Utica

SICILY

Carthage

NUMIDIA

Syrac

Hadrumetum

MELITA

Thapsus

Me

Alexander the Great

Sabrata

Olea Leptis

EMPIRE OF ALEXANDER THE GREAT
(late 4th century B.C.)

16

MACEDONIA

Pella

Black Sea

Aral Sea

Athens

Sardes

Caspian Sea

Sparta

Maracanda

Bactra Derbent

Mediterranean

Drapsaca

Sea Thapcasus

Nisibis Gaugamela

Meshed

Massaga

SYRIA Arbela

Alexandria Tyre Damascus

Rhagae

Cabura

Ammonium

Babylon Ecbatana

Kandahar

Memphis Heliopolis Susa PERSIA

Jerusalem Persepolis

Charax

EGYPT

Golashkerd Pura

ARABIA

Patala

Red Sea

Greek
sphere

| 0 | 400 | 800 miles |

| 0 | 400 | 800 km |

/// Former Persian Empire

Alexander's Empire

→ Routes taken by Alexander's army

Cities founded by Alexander

© carta

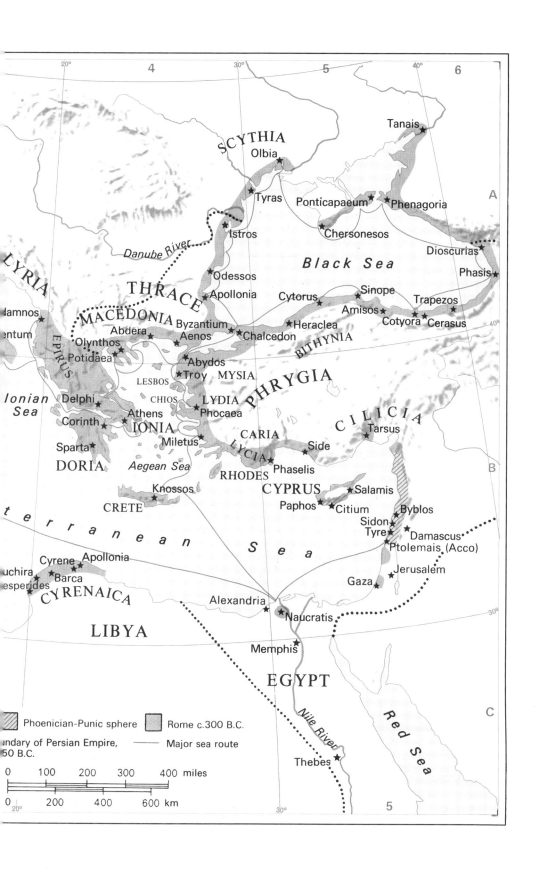

4   20°   30°   **5**   40°   **6**

SCYTHIA

Tanais ★

Olbia ★

Tyras ★   Ponticapaeum ★ ★Phenagoria   A

Istros ★   Chersonesos ★   Dioscurias ★

Danube River   *Black Sea*   Phasis ★

LYRIA   Odessos ★

THRACE   Apollonia ★   Cytorus ★   Sinope ★   Trapezos ★

lamnos ★   MACEDONIA   Byzantium ★   Amisos ★   Cotyora ★★Cerasus

entum   Abdera ★   Aenos ★ ★Chalcedon   Heraclea ★   40°

Olynthos ★   BITHYNIA

EPIRUS Potidaea ★   Abydos ★

      ★Troy   MYSIA   PHRYGIA

LESBOS

Ionian   Delphi ★   CHIOS   LYDIA   CILICIA

Sea   Athens ★ ★Phocaea   Tarsus ★

Corinth ★   IONIA   CARIA   Side ★   B

Sparta ★   Miletus ★   LYCIA   Phaselis ★

DORIA   *Aegean Sea*   RHODES

Knossos ★   CYPRUS   ★Salamis

CRETE   Paphos ★ ★Citium   Byblos ★

     Sidon ★   Damascus

terranean   Tyre ★ Ptolemais (Acco)

     Sea   Jerusalem ★

Cyrene ★ Apollonia

uchira ★ ★ Barca   Gaza ★

esperides ★ CYRENAICA   Alexandria ★

     ★Naucratis   30°

LIBYA   Memphis ★   C

EGYPT   *Red Sea*

▨ Phoenician-Punic sphere   ▦ Rome c.300 B.C.   *Nile River*

undary of Persian Empire,   —— Major sea route
50 B.C.

Thebes ★

0   100   200   300   400 miles

0   200   400   600 km
   20°   30°   **5**

HIBERNIA

BRITANNIA

North Sea

Eburacum

Lindum

Aquae Sulis

Londinium

Atlantic Ocean

GERMANIA

Rhine River

Lutetia

GALLIA

Regina Castra

Vindob

Mediolanum

Lugdunum

RAETIA

NORICUM

PAN

Burdigala

Vienna

Aquileia

ILLYR

Nemausus

Genua

HISPANIA

Narbo

Massilia

ITALIA

Toletum

Tarraco

Ancona

Corduba

Valentia

Rome

Gades

Neapolis

Brundisiu

MAURETANIA

Hippo Regius

AFRICA

Carthage

Syracuse

Medite

ROME (1st-3rd centuries A.D.)

Leptis Magna

Circus of Hadrian

Tomb of Augustus

PINCIAN HILL

Castra Praetoria

Mausoleum of Hadrian

QUIRINAL HILL

Baths of Diocletian

Circus of Nero

VATICAN HILL

Pantheon

VIMINAL HILL

Theater of Pompey

Imperial Fora

ESQUILINE HILL

CAPITOLINE HILL

Capitol Roman Forum

Baths of Trajan

PALATINE HILL

Colosseum

Circus Maximus

T. Divi Claudii

CAELIAN HILL

AVENTINE HILL

Baths of Caracalla

✚ Earliest Christian sites

0   500   1000   1500 yards

0   500   1000 m

© carta

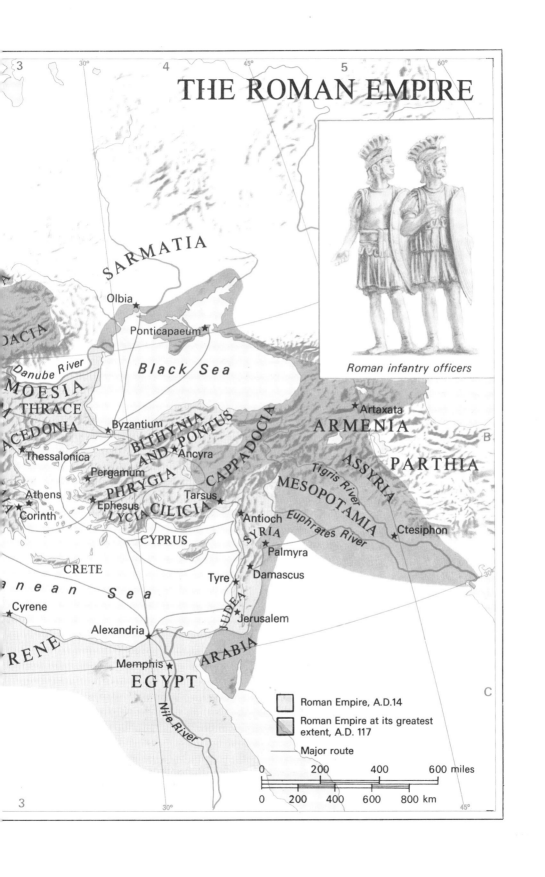

THE ROMAN EMPIRE

Roman infantry officers

SARMATIA

Olbia

Ponticapaeum

Black Sea

DACIA

Danube River

MOESIA

THRACE

ACEDONIA

Thessalonica

Byzantium

BITHYNIA AND PONTUS

Ancyra

Pergamum

PHRYGIA

Athens

Ephesus

LYCIA CILICIA

Corinth

CAPPADOCIA

Tarsus

CYPRUS

CRETE

Artaxata

ARMENIA

PARTHIA

ASSYRIA

MESOPOTAMIA

Tigris River

Antioch

SYRIA

Euphrates River

Ctesiphon

Palmyra

Tyre

Damascus

anean Sea

Cyrene

JUDEA

Jerusalem

Alexandria

CRENE

ARABIA

Memphis

EGYPT

Nile River

	Roman Empire, A.D.14
	Roman Empire at its greatest extent, A.D. 117
	Major route

| 0 | 200 | 400 | 600 miles |

| 0 | 200 | 400 | 600 | 800 km |

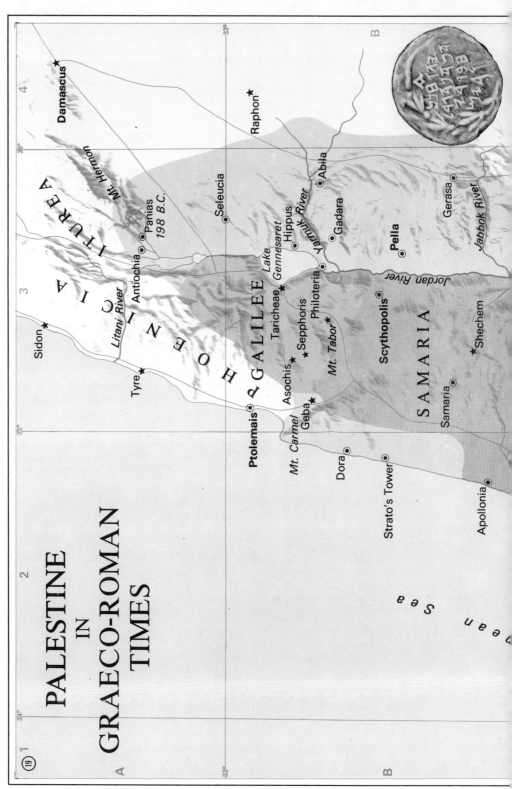

PALESTINE
IN
GRAECO-ROMAN
TIMES

Damascus

Raphon

Mt. Hermon

ITUREA

Panias
198 B.C.

Seleucia

Abila

Antiochia

Litani River

PHOENICIA

Gerasa

Jabbok River

Gadara

Pella

Sidon

Lake
Gennesaret

Hippus

Yarmuk River

Jordan River

Tyre

GALILEE

Taricheae

Sepphoris

Philoteria

Asochis

Mt. Tabor

Scythopolis

SAMARIA

Ptolemais

Mt. Carmel

Geba

Shechem

Samaria

Dora

Strato's Tower

Apollonia

...ean Sea

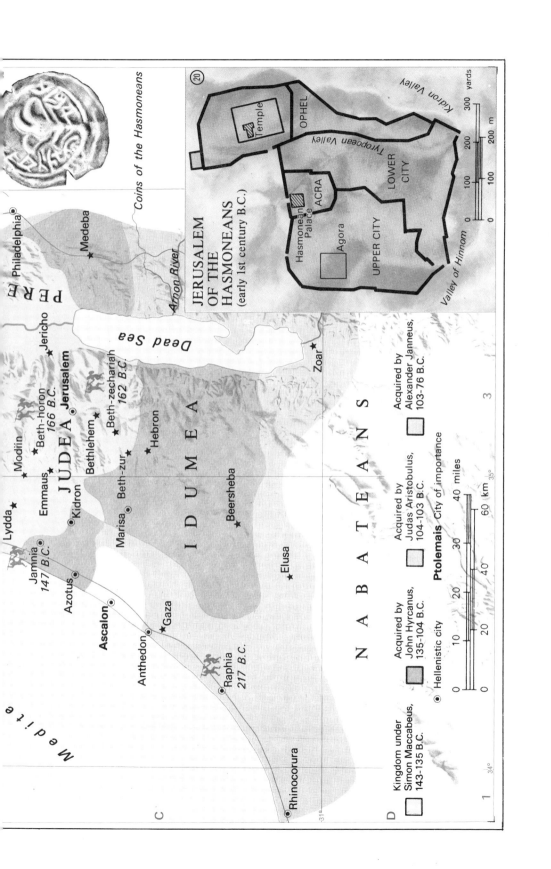

Coins of the Hasmoneans

JERUSALEM
OF THE
HASMONEANS
(early 1st century B.C.)

Temple

OPHEL

Kidron Valley

Tyropoean Valley

Hasmonean Palace

ACRA

LOWER CITY

Agora

UPPER CITY

Valley of Hinnom

0   100   200   300 yards

0   100   200 m

Philadelphia

Medeba

Armon River

P E R E

Jericho

Dead Sea

Beth-horon
166 B.C.

Modiin

Jerusalem

JUDEA

Beth-zechariah
162 B.C.

Bethlehem

Emmaus

Beth-zur

Hebron

Kidron

Marisa

I D U M E A

Lydda

Jamnia
147 B.C.

Azotus

Ascalon

Gaza

Anthedon

Beersheba

Zoar

Elusa

Raphia
217 B.C.

N A B A T E A N S

Rhinocorura

M e d i t e

Kingdom under
Simon Maccabeus,
143-135 B.C.

Acquired by
John Hyrcanus,
135-104 B.C.

Acquired by
Judas Aristobulus,
104-103 B.C.

Acquired by
Alexander Janneus,
103-76 B.C.

Ptolemais City of importance

● Hellenistic city

0   10   20   30   40 miles

0   20   40   60 km   35°

34°

C

D

1

3

31°

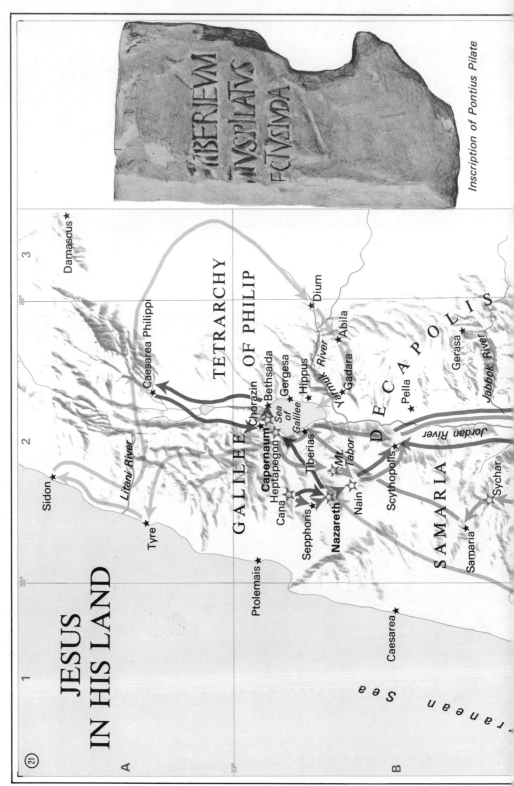

JESUS
IN HIS LAND

Inscription of Pontius Pilate

TIBEREVM
...NTIVS PILATVS
...ECTVSIVDA

Damascus ★

3

Caesarea Philippi ★

TETRARCHY

OF PHILIP

GALILEE

Chorazin ★
Bethsaida ★
Capernaum ★ Gergesa
Heptapegon Hippus ★
Sea of
Galilee
Cana ★ Tiberias ★
Sepphoris ★ Mt.
Nazareth ★ Tabor ☆
Nain ☆

Dium ★

Yarmuk River
Gadara ★ Abila ★

D E C A P O L I S

Pella ★

Gerasa ★
Jabbok River

Jordan River

Sidon ★

Litani River

Tyre ★

Scythopolis ☆

S A M A R I A

Samaria ★

Sychar ★

Ptolemais ★

Caesarea ★

Mediterranean Sea

A

B

1

2

35°
36°
33°

㉑

© carta

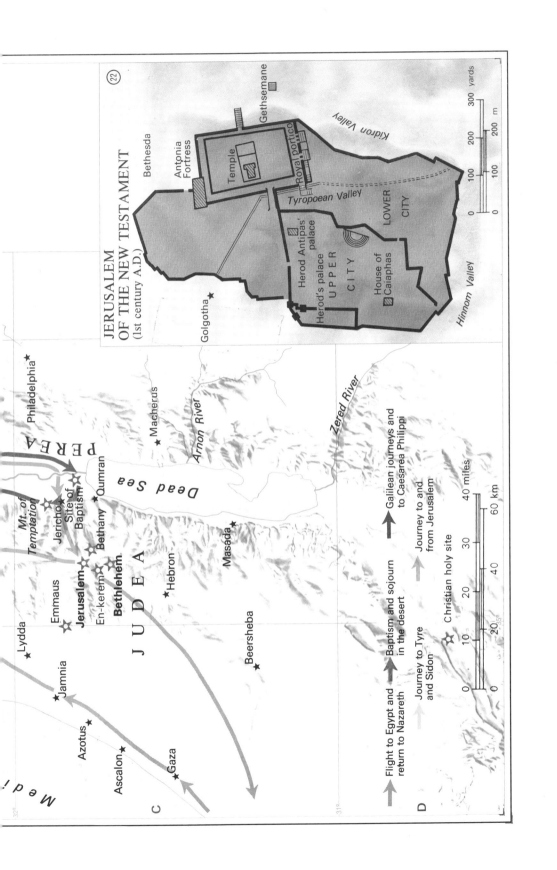

JERUSALEM
OF THE NEW TESTAMENT
(1st century A.D.)

Bethesda

Antonia
Fortress

Temple

Royal Portico

Gethsemane

Kidron Valley

Tyropoean Valley

Herod Antipas'
palace

Herod's palace

UPPER
CITY

LOWER
CITY

House of
Caiaphas

Golgotha

Hinnom Valley

300 yards

200 m

Philadelphia

Macherus

Arnon River

Zered River

Mt. of
Temptation

PEREA

Jericho

Site of
Baptism

Bethany

Qumran

Dead Sea

Lydda

Emmaus

Jamnia

Jerusalem

En-kerem

Bethlehem

JUDEA

Hebron

Masada

Azotus

Ascalon

Beersheba

Gaza

Flight to Egypt and
return to Nazareth

Baptism and sojourn
in the desert

Galilean journeys and
to Caesarea Philippi

Journey to and
from Jerusalem

Journey to Tyre
and Sidon

Christian holy site

40 miles

60 km

Medi

C

D

22

31°

35°

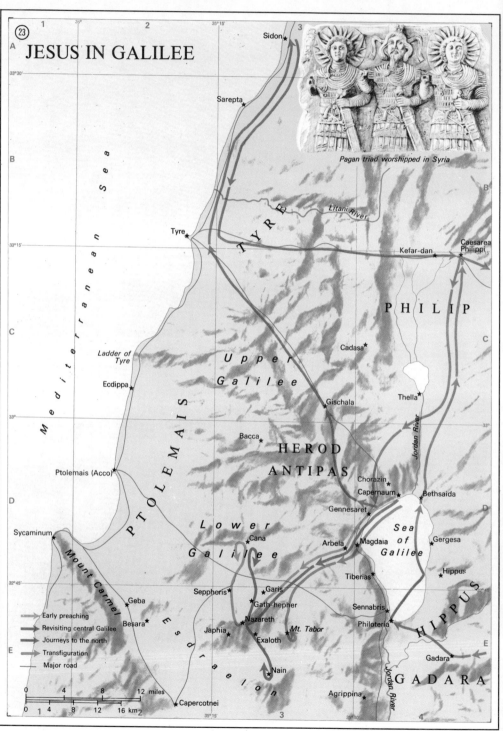

JESUS IN GALILEE

㉓

Sidon

Sarepta

Pagan triad worshipped in Syria

Litani River

TYRE

Tyre

Caesarea Philippi

Kefar-dan

PHILIP

Mediterranean Sea

Cadasa

Upper Galilee

Ladder of Tyre

Thella

Ecdippa

Gischala

Jordan River

Bacca

HEROD ANTIPAS

Ptolemais (Acco)

Chorazin

Capernaum

Bethsaida

PTOLEMAIS

Gennesaret

Lower Galilee

Cana

Sea of Galilee

Sycaminum

Arbela

Magdaia

Gergesa

Mount Carmel

Tiberias

Hippus

Sepphoris

Garis

Gath-hepher

Geba

Nazareth

Sennabris

HIPPUS

Besara

Japhia

Mt. Tabor

Philoteria

Exaloth

Esdraelon

Early preaching
Revisiting central Galilee
Journeys to the north
Transfiguration
Major road

Nain

Gadara

0   4   8   12 miles
0 1 4   8   12   16 km

Agrippina

Jordan River

GADARA

Capercotnei

© carta

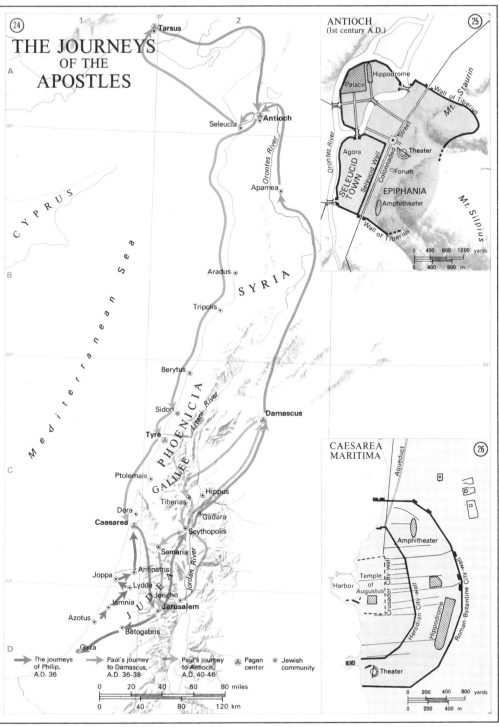

THE JOURNEYS
OF THE
APOSTLES

Tarsus

35°

A

36°

Seleucia **Antioch**

Apamea

C Y P R U S

Orontes River

Aradus

S Y R I A

B

Tripolis

M e d i t e r r a n e a n   S e a

34°

Berytus

Sidon

Litani River

Damascus

P H O E N I C I A

Tyre

G A L I L E E

Ptolemais

C

Hippus

Dora

Tiberias

Caesarea

Gadara

Scythopolis

Samaria

Jordan River

Joppa

Antipatris

30°

Lydda

Jericho

Jamnia

Jerusalem

J U D E A

Azotus

Betogabris

Gaza

D

→ The journeys
of Philip,
A.D. 36

→ Paul's journey
to Damascus,
A.D. 36-38

→ Paul's journey
to Antioch,
A.D. 40-46

△ Pagan
center

⊛ Jewish
community

0	20	40	60	80 miles
0	40	80	120 km	

ANTIOCH
(1st century A.D.)

Hippodrome

Palace

Wall of Tiberius

Mt. Staurin

Orontes River

Agora

Seleucid Wall

Theater

Colonnaded Street

Forum

SELEUCID TOWN

EPIPHANIA

Amphitheater

Wall of Tiberius

Mt. Silpius

0	400	800	1200 yards
0	400	800 m	

CAESAREA
MARITIMA

Aqueduct

Amphitheater

Temple
of
Augustus

Harbor

Crusader City-wall

Herodian City-wall

Hippodrome

Roman-Byzantine City-wall

Theater

0	200	400	600 yards
0	200	400 m	

© carta

Map 27

	1	2	3

A

Rome
ITALY
SARDINIA
Puteoli
Carales
THRACE
MACEDONIA **Philippi**
Beroea **Thessalonica** Nicomedi
Troy
ACHAIA Assos
PH
Pergamum
Delphi
Athens Sardes A:
Corinth Eleusis **Ephesus**
LYC

B

Carthage
SICILY
Rhegium
Syracuse

MELITA

CRETE RHOD
Lasea **Salmone**

Mediterranean Sea

Cyrene
CYRENAICA

Map 28 — PAUL'S MISSION[S]

Rome
Puteoli
Philippi
Beroea
Troy
Assos
Delphi
Corinth Athens
Ephesus
Antioch
Lystra Derbe
Attalia Tarsus
Antioch
Rhegium
Syracuse
Salamis
Mediterranean Sea
Lasea Salmone
Paphos
Damasc
Tyre
Cyrene
Caesarea
Jerusalem
Alexandria

→ Paul's first
missionary journey,
A.D. 46–48.

→ Paul's second
missionary journey,
A.D. 49–52.

→ Paul's third
missionary journey,
A.D. 53–57.

→ Paul's journey to Rome,
A.D. 59–62.

0	100	200
0	100	200 km

© carta

Black Sea

Sinope

BITHYNIA
AND PONTUS

Ancyra

GALATIA

CAPPADOCIA

ADIABENE

PARTHIA

PISIDIA

Nisibis

Hamadan

Antioch
Lystra
Perge
Attalia

Iconium
Derbe

CILICIA

Tarsus

Antioch

Euphrates River

Tigris River

Seleucia

atara

CYPRUS

Salamis

SYRIA

Dora

Ctesiphon

Susa

Paphos

Pumbeditha
Nehardea

Sidon
Tyre

Damascus

Ptolemais

Caesarea

Jerusalem

JUDEA

Alexandria

GYPT

Nile River

Red Sea

THE SPREAD
OF THE
EARLY CHURCH

B

C

☐ Area of earliest Christian concentrations

☐ Area of Jewish settlement

⏤ Pagan center

0   100   200   300   400 miles

0   200   400   600 km

*Merchant ship
of Roman period*

THE GROWTH
OF
CHRISTIANITY

(29)

IX

VIII

VIII

VII

Eburacum

Lindum

IV

Londinium

Colonia
Agrippina

Danube River

V

Lugdunum

Vienna

Arelate

Massilia

Salonae

V

Rome

Corduba

Puteoli

256
Carthage

Syracuse

M e d i t e r

Extent of Christian church,
A.D. 1st cent.

Extent of Christian church,
A.D. 2nd cent.

⚔ Notable early church

⊕ Major church council
431 (with date)

IV Century of conversion
to Christianity

COPTS Monophysite church
after 431

········· Boundary of Roman Empire

|||||||| Split of Latin (western) and
Greek (eastern) churches,
A.D. 5th cent.

0   200   400   600 miles

0   200   400   600   800 km

© carta

IX

IX

XI

Christian victims in the arena

Black Sea

Sinope

Anchialus
Amastris
Amisos

Adrianopolis
Constantinople *381*
Melitene

Philippi
Chalcedon
Nicomedia
ARMENIANS

Beroea
451
Nicaea
Samosata

Nicopolis
Pergamum
325
Edessa
Nisibis

ame
Sardes
Tarsus

Athens
Antioch

Aegina
Ephesus
Laodicea
Apamea
Dura
431
Europos

Knossos
Salamis
Tigris River

Paphos

n e a n   S e a
Tyre
Euphrates River

Cyrene
Caesarea

Alexandria
Jerusalem
49

COPTS

Mt. Sinai

Nile River

Red Sea

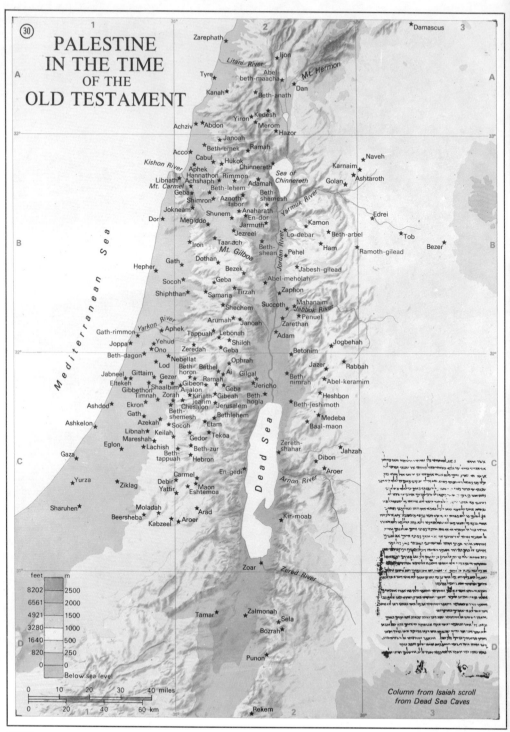

PALESTINE
IN THE TIME
OF THE
OLD TESTAMENT

Mediterranean Sea

Dead Sea

Damascus

Zarephath
Litani River
Ijon
Tyre
Abel-beth-maacha
Mt. Hermon
Kanah
Dan
Beth-anath
Yiron
Kedesh
Achziv
Abdon
Merom
Hazor
Janoah
Acco
Beth-emek
Ramah
Cabul
Hukok
Chinnereth
Kishon River
Aphek
Karnaim
Naveh
Hannathon
Rimmon
Sea of Chinnereth
Golan
Ashtaroth
Libnath
Achshaph
Adamah
Mt. Carmel
Beth-lehem
Beth-shemesh
Geba
Shimron
Aznoth-tabor
Joknoam
Shunem
Anaharath
Edrei
Dor
Megiddo
En-dor
Jarmuth
Kamon
Jezreel
Lo-debar
Beth-arbel
Taanach
Beth-shean
Pehel
Ham
Tob
Iron
Mt. Gilboa
Ramoth-gilead
Bezer
Hepher
Gath
Dothan
Bezek
Abel-meholah
Jabesh-gilead
Socoh
Geba
Zaphon
Shiphthan
Samaria
Tirzah
Mahanaim
Shechem
Succoth
Jabbok River
Penuel
Arumah
Janoah
Zarethan
Gath-rimmon
Yarkon River
Aphek
Tappuah
Lebonah
Adam
Joppa
Yehud
Zeredah
Geba
Shiloh
Betonim
Jogbehah
Beth-dagon
Ono
Ophrah
Nebellat
Jazer
Rabbah
Lod
Beth-horon
Bethel
Jabneel
Gittaim
Gezer
Ai
Gilgal
Beth-nimrah
Abel-keramim
Eltekeh
Shaalbim
Ramah
Jericho
Gibbethon
Zorah
Aijalon
Geba
Beth-hogla
Heshbon
Timnah
Kiriath-jearim
Gibeah
Ashdod
Ekron
Chesalon
Jerusalem
Beth-jeshimoth
Gath
Beth-shemesh
Bethlehem
Ashkelon
Azekah
Socoh
Etam
Medeba
Libnah
Keilah
Tekoa
Baal-maon
Mareshah
Gedor
Eglon
Lachish
Beth-zur
Zereth-shahar
Jahzah
Gaza
Beth-tappuah
Hebron
Dibon
Aroer
Yurza
Carmel
En-gedi
Arnon River
Ziklag
Debir
Maon
Sharuhen
Yattir
Eshtemoa
Moladah
Arad
Beersheba
Aroer
Kir-moab
Kabzeel

Zoar
Zered River

Tamar
Zalmonah
Sela
Bozrah

Punon

Rekem

feet | m
8202 | 2500
6561 | 2000
4921 | 1500
3280 | 1000
1640 | 500
820 | 250
0 | 0
Below sea level

0   10   20   30   40 miles
0   20   40   60 km

*Column from Isaiah scroll
from Dead Sea Caves*

© carta

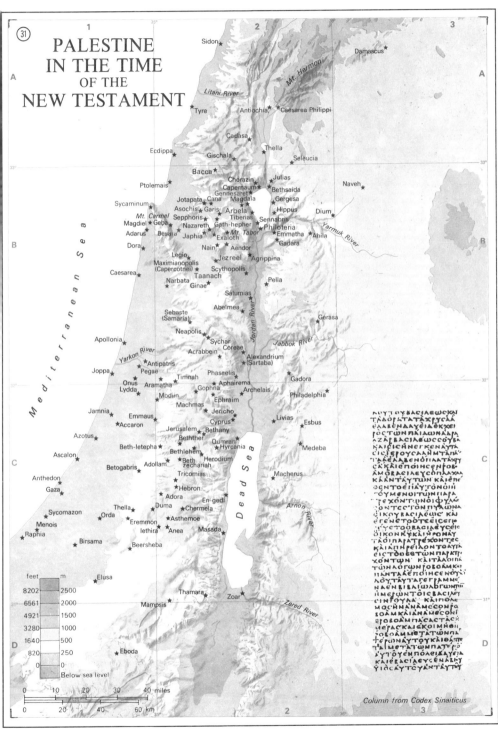

PALESTINE
IN THE TIME
OF THE
NEW TESTAMENT

③

A

Sidon ★

Damascus ★

Mt. Hermon

Litani River

Tyre ★
Antiochia ★   ★ Caesarea Philippi

Cadasa ★

Ecdippa ★
Thella ★
Gischala ★   Seleucia ★

Bacca ★

Chorazin ★   Julias ★
Ptolemais ★   Capernaum ★   ★ Bethsaida
Gennesaret ★   Gergesa ★

Sycaminum ★   Jotapata ★ Cana   Magdala ★
Asochis ★   Garis ★   Arbela ★   Hippus ★   Dium ★
Mt. Carmel   Sepphoris ★   Tiberias ★
Magdiel ★ ★ Geba   Nazareth ★   Gath-hepher ★   Sennabris ★   Naveh ★
Adarus ★   Besara ★   Japhia ★   *Mt. Tabor*   Philoteria ★
Dora ★   Exaloth ★   Emmatha ★   Ahila ★
Nain ★   Aendor ★   Gadara ★
Legio ★   Jezreel ★   Agrippina ★
Maximianopolis ★   Scythopolis ★
(Capercotnei)
Caesarea ★   Taanach ★   Pella ★
Narbata ★   Ginae ★
Salumias ★
Abelmea ★
Sebaste ★   Gerasa ★
(Samaria)
Neapolis ★
Apollonia ★   Sychar ★
Coreae ★
Yarkon River   Acrabbein ★
★ Antipatris   Alexandrium ★
Joppa ★   Pegae ★   Phasaelis ★   (Sartaba)
Onus ★   Timnah ★   Aphairema ★   Gadora ★
Lydda ★   Aramatha ★   Gophna ★   Archelais ★   Philadelphia ★
Modiin ★   Ephraim ★
Jamnia ★   Machmas ★   Jericho ★
Emmaus ★   Cyprus ★   Livias ★   Esbus ★
★ Accaron   Jerusalem ★   Bethany ★
Azotus ★   Bethther ★   Qumran ★   Hyrcania ★   Medeba ★
Ascalon ★   Beth-letepha ★   Bethlehem ★   Herodium ★
Betogabris ★   Adollam ★ Beth   Macherus ★
Anthedon ★   zechariah
Tricomias ★
Gaza ★   Hebron ★
Adora ★   En-gedi ★
Sycomazon ★   Thella ★   Duma ★   Chermela ★   *Arnon River*
Menois ★   Orda ★   Asthemoe ★
Raphia ★   Eremmon ★   Anea ★   Masada ★
Iethira ★
Birsama ★
Beersheba ★

Mediterranean Sea

Jordan River

Jabbok River

Yarmuk River

Dead Sea

Elusa ★

Thamara ★
Mampsis ★   Zoar ★   *Zered River*

Eboda ★

feet	m
8202	2500
6561	2000
4921	1500
3280	1000
1640	500
820	250
0	0
	Below sea level

0   10   20   30   40 miles
0   20   40   60 km

Column from Codex Sinaiticus

© carta

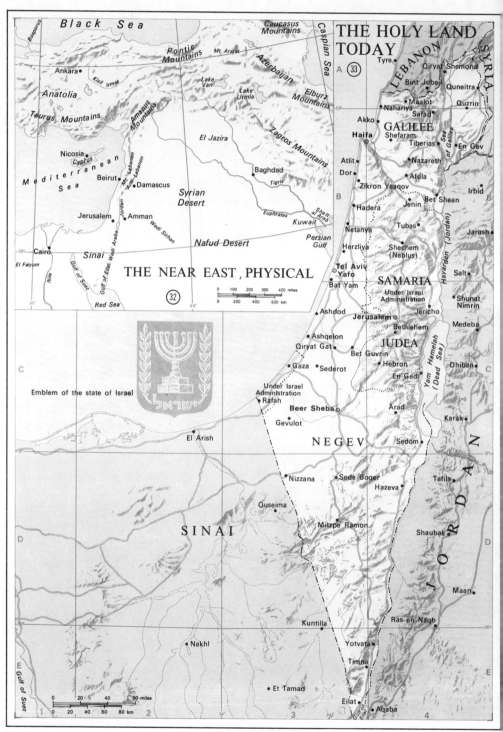

THE HOLY LAND TODAY

A ③③

THE NEAR EAST, PHYSICAL

③②

Black Sea

Bosporus
Pontic Mountains
Mt. Ararat
Caucasus Mountains
Caspian Sea
Ankara
Kizil Irmak
Anatolia
Lake Van
Azerbaijan
Elburz Mountains
Taurus Mountains
Amanus Mountains
El Jazira
Zagros Mountains
Nicosia
Cyprus
Mediterranean Sea
Beirut
Mt. Lebanon
Anti-Lebanon
Damascus
Baghdad
Tigris
Syrian Desert
Jerusalem
Jordan
Amman
Euphrates
Shatt al Arab
Wadi Sirhan
Kuwait
Cairo
Sinai
Nafud Desert
Persian Gulf
El Faiyum
Gulf of Eilat, Wadi Araba
Nile
Gulf of Suez
Red Sea

Emblem of the state of Israel

Tyre
Qiryat Shemona
Bint Jubail
LEBANON
SYRIA
Quneitra
Maalot
Nahariya
Safad
Quzrin
Akko
GALILEE
Haifa
Shefaram
Tiberias
Sea of Galilee
Atlit
Nazareth
En Gev
Dor
Afula
Irbid
Zikron Yaaqov
Bet Shean
Hadera
Jenin
Netanya
Tubas
Jarash
Herzliya
Shechem (Nablus)
Hayarden (Jordan)
Salt
Tel Aviv
Yafo
SAMARIA
Bat Yam
Under Israel Administration
Jericho
Shunat Nimrin
Ashdod
Jerusalem
Medeba
Ashqelon
Bethlehem
Qiryat Gat
JUDEA
Yam Hamelah (Dead Sea)
Gaza
Bet Guvrin
Dhiban
Sederot
Hebron
Under Israel Administration
En Gedi
Rafah
Karak
Beer Sheba
Arad
Gevulot
Sedom
El Arish
NEGEV
Nizzana
Sede Boqer
Tafila
Hazeva
Quseima
Mitzpe Ramon
Shaubak
SINAI
Kuntilla
Ras en Naqb
Nakhl
Yotvata
Timna
J O R D A N
Maan
Et Tamad
Eilat
Aqaba
Gulf of Eilat
Gulf of Suez

0   100 200 300 400 miles
0   200   400   600 km

0   20   40   60 miles
0 20 40 60 80 km

© carta

INDEX   Map numbers (not page references) are used in the following index

A

Assos 27 B3; 28
Asthemoe 31 C2
Athens 2 B1; 5 B1; 15 B4; 16; 17 B3;
    27 B3; 28; 29 B3
Atlantic Ocean 17 A1
Atlit 33 B3
Attalia 27 B4; 28
Azekah 9 C1; 30 C1
Azerbaijan 32
Aznoth-tabor 30 B2
Azotus (see Ashdod)

B

Baal-maon 30 C2
Babylon 2 C5; 3 C5; 5 C5; 6; 16
Babylonia 3 C6; 5 C5
Bacca 23 D3; 31 B2
Bactra 16
Baghdad 32
Baptism, site of 21 C2
Barak, Judge 9 B2
Barca 15 B4
Bashan 9 A2; 13 B3
Batruna 7 A2
Bat Yam 33 C3
Beersheba 7 D1; 9 C1; 11 D1; 13 D1;
    19 C2; 21 C1; 30 C1; 31 C1
Beirut 32; 33 C3
Benjamin, tribe 9 C2
Beroea 27 A3; 28; 29 B3
Berytus 24 C2
Besara 23 E2; 31 B2
Bet Guvrin (see Betogabris) 33 C3
Beth-anath 30 A2
Bethany 21 C2; 31 C2
Beth-arbel 30 B2
Bethesda 22
Beth-dagon 30 C1
Bethel 9 C2; 11 D2; 13 D2; 30 C2
Beth-emek 30 B2
Beth-haram 7 D2
Beth-hogla 30 C2
Beth-horon 7 D2; 11 D2; 19 C3; 30 C2
Beth-jeshimoth 30 C2
Bethlehem 9 C2; 19 C3; 21 C2; 30 C2; 31 C2
Beth-lehem (in Galilee) 30 B2
Beth-letepha 31 C2
Beth-nimrah 30 C2
Bethsaida 21 B2; 23 B2; 31 B2
Beth-shean 7 C2; 9 B2; 11 C2; 30 B2
Beth-shemesh 11 D2; 30 C1
Beth-shemesh (in Galilee) 30 B2
Beth-tappuah 30 C2
Bethther 31 C2
Beth-zechariah 19 C3; 31 C2
Beth-zur 19 C3; 30 C2
Betogabris 24 D1; 31 C1
Betonim 30 C2
Bet Shean (see also Beth-shean) 33 B4
Bezek 30 B2
Bezer (in Hauran) 7 C3; 30 B3
Bezer (in Moab) 11 D2
Bint Jubail 33 A4

Birsama 31 C1
Bithynia 15 A5
(Bithynia and Pontus) 17 B4; 27 A4
Black Sea 3 A4; 5 A4; 15 A5; 16; 17 B4;
    27 A4; 29 B4
Bosporus 32
Bozrah 7 E2; 9 D2; 11 E2; 13 E2; 30 D2
Britannia 17 A1
Brundisium 17 B3
Brook of Egypt 11 D1
Burdigala 17 B1
Byblos 2 C4; 3 C4; 7 A2; 11 A2; 13 A2; 15 B5
Byzantium 15 A4; 17 B3

C

Cabul 30 B2
Cabura 16
Cadasa (see Kedesh) 23 C4; 31 A2
Caesarea 21 B1; 24 C1; 26; 27 B4; 28;
    29 B4; 31 B1
Caesarea Philippi 21 A2; 23 C4; 31 A2
Cairo 32
Cana 21 B2; 23 D3; 31 B2
Canaan 1; 3 C3; 10
Capercotnei (see Legio Maximianopolis)
    23 E2
Capernaum 21 B2; 23 D4; 31 B2
Caphtorim 1
Cappadocia 17 B4; 27 B4
Carales 15 B2; 27 B1
Carchemish 2 B4; 3 B4; 5 B4
Caria 15 B4
Carmel (in Judea) 30 C2
Carmel, Mt. 7 C2; 9 B2; 11 C2; 13 C2;
    19 B2; 23 D2; 30 B2; 31 B2
Cartenna 15 B2
Carthage 15 B3; 17 B2; 27 B2; 29 B2
Caspian Sea 5 A7; 16
Caucasus Mts. 32
Celts 15 A2
Cerasus 15 A5
Chalcedon 15 A4; 29 B3
Charax 16
Chermela 31 C2
Chersonesos 15 A5
Chesalon 30 C2
Chinnereth 9 B2; 11 C2; 30 B2
Chinnereth, Sea of 7 C2; 9 B2; 11 C2;
    13 C2; 30 B2
Chios 15 B4
Chorazin 21 B2; 23 D4; 31 B2
Cilicia 15 B5; 17 B4; 27 B4
Citium 15 B5
Colonia Agrippina 29 A2
Constantinople 29 B3
Copts 29 B3
Corduba 17 B1; 29 B1
Coreae 31 B2
Corinth 5 B1; 15 B4; 17 B3; 27 B3; 28
Cotyora 15 A5
Crete 2 B1; 5 B1; 15 B4; 17 B3; 27 B3
Croton 15 B3
Ctesiphon 17 B4; 27 B5